HAUNTED
LAKE PLACID

HAUNTED
LAKE PLACID
The Spirits of Essex County

LYNDA LEE MACKEN

HAUNTED LAKE PLACID
The Spirits of Essex County

Published by
Black Cat Press
P. O. Box 1218
Forked River, NJ 08731
www.lyndaleemacken.com

Photo Credits: Library of Congress pages 9, 10, 21, 80, 83, 96, 97 and 101; Green-Wood Cemetery page 15; Mike Delahant page 36; Enesse Bhé photo, licensed under the Creative Commons Attribution-Share Alike 2.0 Generic license, page 67; Wikipedia images pages 77, 79 and 95; Old House Dreams page 89; Wikimedia Commons images page 76 and 100. All other photos by author.

ISBN 978-0-9829580-5-6

Printed in the United States of America by Sheridan Books, Inc.
www.sheridanbooks.com

Book & Cover Design by Deb Tremper, Six Penny Graphics.
www.sixpennygraphics.com

To the Spirit of the
Great North Woods.

CONTENTS

INTRODUCTION

They say of this old, mossy wood,
Whose hoary trunks have for ages stood,
That every knoll and dim-lit glade
Is haunted at night by its restless Shade.
—Isaac McLellan Jr., *The Haunted Wood*

Winter sports and Lake Placid go hand in hand. This cozy alpine village hosted two Olympic Winter Games in 1932 and 1980 but the area is much more than an athletic venue. It's a thriving mountain district where individuals have lived and died—and where some of their souls give the term "community spirit" a whole new meaning.

Haunting encounters occur all over the Adirondacks but the reality of ghostly phenomena thrives in Essex County. Spirits are afoot amid majestic mountains, awesome chasms and splendid lakes. The haunted hinterland encompasses the coast of Lake Champlain to the High Peaks and historic villages in between. Specters of miners and murderers, servants and soldiers, suicides and caretakers join ghostly innkeepers and guests in this scenic region that appeals to the living as well as the undead.

In the shadow of Whiteface Mountain, in the midst of Great Camps built by the rich and sometimes infamous, certain rocky cliffs and ledges stand out on the shores of Lake Placid. Known as Pulpit Rock, these stony faces rise out of the lake and descend into its darkest depths. The body of Mabel Smith Douglass came to rest on an underwater ledge when she drowned in 1963. The sight of a diaphanous form hovering over the lake adds another dimension to her mysterious death. Also, at nearby Camp Hillgarth, a resident spirit there puts a new spin on "designing women."

The cool balsam-scented mountain air benefitted tuberculosis patients at nearby Saranac Lake. Dr. Edward Livingston Trudeau pioneered the place as a health resort in the late 1800s. Robert Louis Stevenson and thousands of other sufferers flocked here for a cure. Many regained their health but far too many did not. Some of their spirits journey from beyond still hoping for a healing. Spirits want their stories told and people want to tell their stories. Such is the case at a former Saranac Lake cure cottage.

The mining industry once flourished in northern New York where mines and forges existed along

Lake Champlain as early as the late 1700s. Eleven minerals were quarried from the territory—iron and garnet the two most important. Revenants are revealed from the region's iron mining industry at the Penfield Homestead Museum and Moriah's Town Hall.

Welcome to landmark lodges, mysterious museums and a phantom filled fort—some of the supernaturally shaded places presented in *Haunted Lake Placid*.

LAKE PLACID

STAGECOACH INN

The spirit-world around this world of sense
Floats like an atmosphere, and everywhere
Wafts through these earthly mists and vapors dense
A vital breath of more ethereal air.
—Henry Wadsworth Longfellow, *Haunted Houses*

Years ago fire devastated the Stagecoach Inn on the Old Military Road. Eventually, the roof collapsed and exposed the interior to the elements. Mary Pat Ormsby felt heartbroken to see the building in such a dismal state because she grew up around the corner and spent many hours adventuring in and around the structure. Fortunately, she and her husband Tony Carlino managed to purchase the then sad property. The couple faced a daunting task, the wooden floor, for instance, was buckled as high as three feet in some places. For over four years, the pair worked carefully and tirelessly to authentically restore the Stagecoach Inn to its original rustic grandeur.

The place started out as a family home. Around 1833, Iddo Osgood opened his doors to travelers and an institution was born. Somewhere along the line a tavern room was added and now the Lyon's Inn became a gathering place for locals who rubbed elbows with out-of-towners. At one time the building housed the post office and was home to Melvil Dewey, the founder of the Lake Placid Club. As the oldest standing structure in Lake Placid,

the inn has witnessed several historical visitors.
Verplank Colvin, Seneca Ray Stoddard and William
Henry Dana, author of *Two Years Before the Mast*, are
some of the inn's noteworthy guests.

Some suspect the Stagecoach Inn is haunted.
Former employees claimed guests spotted spectral
entities or felt their presence. Housekeepers
reported that someone, or some*thing*, swiped
pillowcases. This phantom pilferer took its penchant
for pillows a step beyond. Prior owners used to
display hand-crafted pillows with the message
"Welcome Friends" on the couch. The cushions
would sometimes be found turned around or upside
down when no one else frequented the room.

The Stagecoach Inn possesses a "spirit of place," in contrast to "haunted." I believe the Stagecoach Inn is home to "genius loci," protective spirits. Mary Pat Ormsby is the embodiment of one and the other is less tangible. The owners' restoration created a space for the spirit of place to thrive. Feng shui, and similar practices, re-enchant properties in order to establish, or re-establish, a distinctive atmosphere. At the Stagecoach Inn, Mary Pat's innate sensibilities have done just that—and more. Douglas fir wainscoting, yellow birch bark railings and fireplace trimmings along with select decorative objects, such as old snowshoes and antique skis radiate a distinctive energy. The inn is a time travelers dream for reverting to the 19th century.

I initially wrote about the gently spirited lodge in *Adirondack Ghosts* (2000). During a recent stay at the Stagecoach, I asked Mary Pat if she felt the lodge was haunted. She didn't think so. That night as I reached to turn off my bedside lamp the light shut off before my fingers reached the switch. "Interesting...," I thought.

The next morning, over a scrumptious breakfast, I shared my odd experience with my host. Mary Pat said she'd have Tony look at the light switch. I smiled and told her I thought it might be a ghost. The owner thoughtfully sipped her coffee and recounted a strange incident on the staircase. As she carried a large bundle down the stairs she lost her footing. Bordering on the sickening sensation that precedes a great fall, her descent suddenly came to a halt. Did a pair of invisible hands set her aright? I believe this savior is a grateful entity who appreciates the couple for breathing new life into the old structure. The spirit set Mary Pat's balance back on track much as she did with the landmark inn.

Is the Stagecoach Inn haunted? I'd say it's gently spirited by the presence of the past entwining with the present.

JOHN BROWN FARM

We have no title-deeds to house or lands;
Owners and occupants of earlier dates
From graves forgotten stretch their dusty hands,
And hold in mortmain still their old estates.
—Henry Wadsworth Longfellow, *Haunted Houses*

The John Brown Farm is the final resting place of abolitionist John Brown. The historic property commemorates the man who fought against slavery and created one of the most enduring legends in the nation's history.

In 1849, John Brown moved from Springfield, Massachusetts, where he conducted a stop on the Underground Railroad, to lead freed slaves

in farming in North Elba near Lake Placid. Purchasing a lot from Gerrit Smith, New York's wealthiest abolitionist, Brown moved his family to the wilderness area where he would guide and teach black families farming parcels of land granted to them by Smith. Brown named the settlement *Timbuctoo* in honor of the ancient African city of learning. But when Brown arrived in the Adirondacks he found only a handful of families. Cold winters, lack of supplies, taxes and the harsh mountain landscape discouraged most of the grantees.

Brown moved to Kansas in 1855 where two of his sons led armed revolts against proslavery forces. He returned to his upstate farm six times to visit his wife and some of his children.

On the night of October 16, 1859, Brown and his followers raided the U.S. arsenal at Harper's Ferry to capture firearms for use in a forceful campaign toward slave liberation. Brown was arrested and imprisoned at Charlestown, Virginia, where he was tried and hanged on December 2, 1859. He refused burial in Virginia because he opposed internment in a slave-made coffin. Brown's wife shipped his corpse, first to New York City where an undertaker prepared the body, then on to Essex County.

Inside the Essex County Courthouse hangs a life-size portrait of John Brown's trial for the failed raid at Harper's Ferry. Brown's body lay in state in the courthouse on the night of December 6, 1859 on its way to burial at his farm. Soon after Brown's death his homestead became a pilgrimage site for free African Americans and white abolitionists.

Ultimately the experimental community declined due to its remote location and harsh climate. In due course, Brown's family moved to California at the onset of the Civil War. In 1870, the John Brown Association purchased the farm and gravesite. The State of New York received ownership in 1896.

Linda Roy is the historic site's interpreter and has led tours of John Brown's farmhouse for over 20 summer seasons. While researching the location's history, Linda discovered her great, great grandmother, Elizabeth Reed, also worked at the Brown farm during the summer months decades earlier. Undoubtedly, this ancestral connection explains Linda's strong attachment to the property along with her intuitive gifts which add an especially extraordinary dimension.

When the Hughes family farmed the land a hundred years ago, their son, Billy, died from a lightning strike while plowing a field. Linda discerned his presence during her fourth year at the farm. The interpreter spotted Billy at the foot of the cellar stairs looking up at her. His form glowed with a reddish aura. Is this glow a postmortem after effect of a lightning strike? On another occasion she spied his silhouette standing in the root cellar. Some visitors sight Billy's phantom form standing at the living room window.

John Brown's daughter-in-law Martha passed away soon after giving birth to daughter Olive. The child passed on shortly thereafter. When downstairs, Linda often discerns the movement of the rocking chair overhead. The docent feels the sound is the devoted mother's spirit carrying on her maternal duties.

The John Brown Farm is a documented site on New York's Underground Railroad Heritage Trail. It is located slightly off the beaten track on John Brown Road, south of the intersection with Old Military Road in Lake Placid. The tranquil enclave evokes a time gone by for visitors to enjoy along with the spirits who still linger there.

PULPIT ROCK

I have ridden the wind,
I have ridden the night,
I have ridden the ghosts that flee
From the vaults of death like a chilling breath
Over eternity.
—Cale Young Rice, *The Mystic*

On September 15, 1963 two divers discovered a woman's body sixty feet from Pulpit Rock. At first they thought the figure was a mannequin but when they grabbed the arm and the limb easily released from the body, they realized they found a corpse. An investigation quickly identified the woman as Mabel Smith Douglass who disappeared 30 years earlier.

Mabel Smith Douglass was no ordinary woman. Born in Jersey City to a successful merchant, she married an equally prosperous businessman. Accomplishment enough for most women of her generation, Douglass possessed greater ambition. Douglass attended Barnard College and graduated in 1899 with a Phi Beta Kappa key. She possessed a burning desire to establish a woman's college, particularly a companion school to Rutgers, the New Jersey State University. Douglass' single-minded pursuit of this objective took a back seat in 1915 due to frail health. The following year her husband passed away and she was left to raise two small children and run the family business singlehandedly.

Despite these new challenges, Douglass realized her dream two years later, with the establishment of the New Jersey College for Women where she received appointment as the school's first dean.

Her career flourished for five years at the college where Douglass became a legend in her own time. *Beyond* dedicated, the dean devoted countless hours to her vocation and the young women's welfare. Sometimes she worked late into the night at the school and slept on a cot.

On September 9, 1923 disaster struck when her son William committed suicide by shooting himself in their home. Numerous achievements followed the terrible loss, however. Douglass received an honorary doctorate of law the next year. Thanks in large part to her efforts, Voorhees Chapel opened on campus. She was appointed to the New Jersey State Board of Education and in 1930 became the first female recipient of Columbia University's medal for distinguished public service. In 1932 Russell Sage College presented her with an honorary doctorate degree and she was named *Officier d'Academie* by France for promoting French language education in the United States.

Ultimately however, her grueling work ethic triggered a nervous breakdown. Douglass took a leave of absence from the college and voluntarily committed herself to a private psychiatric hospital where she remained for one year. Upon her release, Douglass resigned from the college and retreated to her Camp Onondaga on Lake Placid.

On the last day of her stay at her Adirondack refuge, neighbors observed Douglass board her skiff to pick colorful fall leaves as she informed her daughter. She rowed directly across the lake to Pulpit Rock, notoriously the deepest part of the lake. Some say the water's depth is fathomless.

Later, two workmen claimed they saw her standing in the skiff with a veil over her head and said she threw something into the water and followed after it overturning the boat. They raced to help and noticed the oars neatly tucked under the seats but found no trace of the woman. Douglass' death is ruled an accident.

Thirty years later, *almost to the day*, her body was found. Due to the frigid water temperature and chemical salts in the water, Douglass' fatty body tissue virtually turned to soap by a process called saponification. When her body was removed from its underwater resting-place and exposed to the air, the flesh fell away from the bones.

Her remains were interred in the family plot next to her husband and her son. Strangely enough, Douglass' daughter Edith also suffered the death of her husband at an early age and like her brother, Edith eventually committed suicide.

This tale of triumph and tragedy deepens with reports of a female apparition hovering over the water near Pulpit Rock. The stories began to circulate after Douglass' corpse arose from its frigid resting place. Especially prevalent on autumn evenings, boaters and campers see a nebulous female form floating over Lake Placid. Who is haunting Pulpit Rock? Some are certain it's Mabel S. Douglass unable to rest since her peaceful sleep was disturbed in 1963.

In 1955, the New Jersey College for Women was officially renamed Douglass College in honor of its founder. Students speculate Douglass haunts the campus' Little Theater where they witness the spirit of an older woman playing the piano. Sometimes they hear her voice singing along to the music as well. It's reasonable to suggest that a woman *so* devoted to the places she loved in life would continue to haunt them in death.

LAKE PLACID CLUB

In the quiet, dusky chamber,
By the flickering firelight,
Rising up between two sleepers,
Comes a spirit all in white.
—Louisa May Alcott, *Our Little Ghost*

The Lake Placid Club once stood as the centerpiece of the Village of Lake Placid. In 1891, Melvil Dewey and his wife relocated to Lake Placid for health reasons (Dewey suffered from hay fever). Recognizing the area's potential as a winter sports destination, Dewey purchased five acres on east Mirror Lake and established the Lake Placid Club for visitors to enjoy wintry activities and rejuvenate in the unique restorative locale. The recreational and social club initially attracted intellectual types, including clergy.

As a youth, Dewey preached the evils of wasting time. While attending Amherst College he abhorred the alphabetical arrangement of books because searching for titles took up too much time. Therefore he developed the classification system for books that bears his name—the Dewey Decimal System. Dewey served as the Librarian for Columbia University and the State of New York as well as Secretary of the State Board of Regents.

Some place names in Lake Placid's vicinity possess peculiar phonetic spellings attributed to Dewey who considered eliminating superfluous letters another time-saving device. The Adirondak Loj (loj is pronounced "lodge") is a popular hostel maintained by the Adirondack Mountain Club and one example of Dewey's philosophy of simplified spelling.

The Lake Placid Club initially struggled financially but eventually grew to encompass 9,600 acres. The property holding encompassed an area that extended from Lake Placid Village, beyond the Olympic ski jumps to the High Peaks Wilderness Area on Route 73. By 1923, the club employed over 1,100 and boasted 356 buildings. The enterprise included a dairy, poultry farms, lecture hall, 21 tennis courts and seven golf courses. The 1929 Depression sounded the death knell for the enterprise and in the years that followed the club continued to decline.

Dewey's vision initiated the winter sports craze in Lake Placid. After Dewey's death in 1931, the torch passed to his son Godfrey who became president of the 1932 Lake Placid Winter Olympic Committee. Hosting the Olympics did little to bolster the failing Lake Placid Club.

During World War II, the U.S. Army operated a rehabilitation facility at the onerous resort. When renovations required to repurpose the buildings began, so did the haunting activity. Since energy cannot be destroyed it's theorized that energy emitted during a lifetime somehow embeds itself on the environment. Changes to the physical structure, such as remodeling, somehow wakes up the residual energy left behind by those who once occupied the place. Rehabbing the building brought Annie Dewey back to life, so to speak. Workers witnessed her apparition placidly relaxing in a rocking chair in the library. Is there a better place for the ghost of a librarian's wife to appear? Night watchmen alleged Annie's apparition drifted through the farthest reaches of the cavernous club including the chapel. Annie appeared to go about her day as if she never left.

Lake Placid Club, Florida

In 1926, Melvin and Annie Dewey founded a second Lake Placid Club in Lake Stearns, Florida. Dewey convinced town leaders to change the town's name to Lake Placid. He died there on December 26, 1931, just a few weeks before the opening ceremony for the 1932 Olympic Winter Games in Lake Placid, New York. In the fall of 2011, Lake Placid, New York and Lake Placid, Florida, were joined together in a proclamation as Sister Cities. The two towns share a long tradition of cultural, historical and *mystical* connections.

Annie also haunted the Lake Placid Club in Florida according to Francis Sheffield, a former security guard at the club. Sheffield worked for 23 years at the club during the 1940s and 1960s and said that whenever Annie's specter showed up he would be extra careful because on those occasions something "bad" would happen. One night after his patrol, as Sheffield chatted with the night clerk in the reception area, they heard a terrible crash upstairs. He grabbed his shotgun and headed toward the noise. Unlocking the public relations room, he and the assistant found every book, previously neatly stacked in the room, all over the floor. According to Sheffield, no one could have passed the pair to get to the room—the workers would have seen them.

On further occasions, Sheffield and other guards witnessed Annie's apparition a number of times and described the vision as "somewhat solid, but kind of misty." Several times the elevator made trips between floors when no guests were present and no one got on or off. Also, strange lights sometimes appeared outside the dining room. The dining room existed near the Founder's Room where a portrait of Annie hung on the wall. Sheffield recalled Annie's gaze seemed to follow whoever was present in the room. During the month of February a group of guests known as the "Febs," conducted séances in the sealed room. Sheffield said it's uncertain whether or not they conjured up a ghost. Seems like they might have!

MARION'S SPIRIT

The rooms look just as I left them,
benign, deliberate, even tidy:
the chairs and tables parked properly,
the angles as right as ninepence.
—Bill Greenwell, *Poltergeist*

An entry in the August 20, 1935 issue of *The New York Times* read:

"Mrs. Marion BLOGETT died in hospital near Martigny [Switzerland] from car accident which cost the life of DR W. Beran Wolfe, New York Psychiatrist."

Marion Hilliard Blodgett was the wife of Delos A. Blodgett II, of New York City and Lake Placid. Her funeral was held at the Lake Placid Community Church. Marion, who was 33, died in Martigny, Switzerland, August 19, 1935 from injuries received in an automobile accident four days earlier. She was survived by her husband and two daughters, among other family members.

Enter former Lake Placid resident, the late
Marilyn "Lyn" Witte. Lyn used to manage White
Pine Camp, Calvin Coolidge's 1926 summer White
House, in Paul Smiths. At one time she lived in a
magnificent house on the shores of Lake Placid—
Camp Hillgarth. Many years ago, Lyn invited her
widowed father to live with her in the most perfect
house she had found on the lake. And so began an
extraordinary adventure.

Lyn and her father were the fourth owners of
the grand residence. Six bedrooms, six baths, a
huge entry hall with a center staircase, massive
living room, eight fireplaces, servant quarters, large
boathouse—these were a few of the particulars
of their new home. "The minute I saw it, I knew
I had to have it," she said. Fortunately, they also
"inherited" the caretaker, the late Victor Lefebvre.
Lefebvre worked for the original owners and knew
no other employment.

Lyn waxed nostalgic about her home and went
on to say that Delos A. Blodgett II, son of a lumber
baron and financier, had the residence built on Lake
Placid as a summer home in the 1920s. His wife,
Marion, possessed a discerning eye for design and
oversaw the creation of her new home both inside
and out. She was a woman with style who knew
what she wanted and left no detail to chance.

Lyn and her dad purchased the house fully furnished. "There was furniture everywhere," she said. An avid decorator herself, in this space Lyn felt strong urges to change the location of the furnishings. For instance, a sofa in the boathouse seemed to belong in the living room; downstairs furniture fit better in the bedrooms. Her discriminating taste went beyond her innate knowledge of good design. Lyn claimed she felt *compelled* to position particular pieces in certain spots.

Lyn and Lefebvre worked together moving the objects but after a while the caretaker began to act differently toward the new owner. Lyn sensed something wrong and approached him about his odd behavior. "Oh nothing's wrong ma'am. It's just that you're moving every piece of furniture *exactly* where Mrs. Blodgett had placed it when she lived here."

Lyn was floored, though not deterred. She continued to intuitively replicate Marion's style without exactly understanding why. In fact, one day she felt compulsively drawn to the attic where she couldn't search fast enough to find whatever it was she was looking for. Drawn to a dark corner, she discovered a magnificent Chippendale style mirror. Lyn practically flew down the stairs and directly to the first floor where she placed the attractive mirror against a bare wall. To her amazement she detected the faint outline of where the looking glass hung sixty years before.

Lyn eventually learned that Marion finished arranging her new home around Christmastime. Like most families, the holidays were a special occasion. In fact, Marion and Delos' engagement was announced during the Christmas holidays nearly two decades earlier. With the house now complete, Mr. and Mrs. Blodgett arranged for a well-deserved trip to Europe. Marion never returned to her beloved lakeside retreat due to her fatal car accident.

It was autumn when Lyn and her dad moved into the dwelling. Their new house transformed into a comfortable and pleasing home by following Lyn's inner promptings. The holidays were fast approaching and the house needed decoration and sprucing up for Christmas. One weekend Lyn urged a friend to put up the tree. Well, not exactly *the* tree—Lyn sensed they needed *eight* trees! With much time and effort they trimmed all the trees. At last Lyn gained a peaceful sense of satisfaction especially with their *piéce de résistance,* a two-story beauty that soared in the entry hall.

When Lefebvre returned to work on Monday, Lyn couldn't wait to show off her festive creations. He stood in astonishment and shook his head in wonder. "Mrs. Blodgett put up *eight* trees . . . in *exactly* the same places you have them."

From that moment on, Lyn never again felt the sense of an unseen hand orchestrating her projects. She is convinced the work she accomplished in the home met with the satisfaction of its original designer and ultimate woman of the house Marion Blodgett.

WHITEFACE CLUB

Ghosts ain't things we are apt to fear;
Spirits don't fool with levers much,
And throttle-valves don't take to such.
—Francis Bret Harte, *The Ghost That Jim Saw*

In 1892, the Whiteface Club was built on the
southwest cove of Lake Placid. Called the
Westside, the lodge housed summer guests. In 1898,
the Whiteface Club and Resort was born. At the
time, a popular trend suggested the Adirondack's
balsam-scented air promoted good health. The
region flourished with newcomers as did the grand
hotel.

The Knollwood Cottage overlooks Lake Placid
and exists on the Whiteface Club property. Disaster
struck in 1908 when fire damaged the cottage.
Bickford family members, who built the original
edifice and worked as on-site caretakers, overhauled
the lodge. Another inferno claimed the structure in
1917 and again the Bickfords were there to rebuild.
Yet a third blaze ruined Knollwood and this time
the Bickfords not only reconstructed the building,

they raised more cottages, a convention hall and an 18-hole golf course. Golfers enjoyed the sport at the resort before its official recognition as an Olympic game.

The Bickfords are an institution when it comes to property management. Their caretaking tradition extended to the next generation of five sons who grew up on the premises and witnessed the property develop into a sophisticated and luxurious resort. One son in particular devoted himself to the parcel of prime real estate and all the dwellings his family painstakingly crafted and maintained. Preston Bickford possessed a deep and abiding love for the place.

Preston spent his entire life, with the exception of the war years, working for the Whiteface Inn Company. He tended to everything and eventually became the head plumber. But the times they were a-changing… In 1980 the main lodge was demolished to clear the way for modern condominiums. Preston stood on a nearby hill, leaned against his 1953 Willy's Jeep and sobbed as the structure crumbled. Preston hated change. In fact, his resistance to change precipitated his suicide. That's when strange events began to occur at the Whiteface Club.

Jim Patterson apprenticed to Preston and they were also best friends. With Preston gone, Jim advanced to the head plumber position. Their close relationship is the reason why Jim feels Preston's spirit continues to assist him from beyond the grave. For instance, when Jim ponders over a problem, he'll step back from the job and sense a telepathic suggestion from his departed friend. When he regards the project again, he sees the situation in a way that makes perfect sense.

But the departed plumber's presence is not always so helpful. Preston spent most of his time working in Convention Hall. One morning Jim turned the heating system on in the building and noticed water seeping through the ceiling. With great difficulty, he traced the source of the leak to under the stage where a plug went missing from the pipe. Who could have possibly dislodged the stopper? Jim needed to dismantle the stage structure and crawl 25 feet underneath to repair the leak. After he made the repair, Jim found the errant plug sitting on a ledge behind the pipe. There could only be one explanation. Jim felt certain Preston's phantom played the destructive prank.

The resort's manager-on-duty stays overnight on-site in the event of an emergency. Maintenance manager, Pete Harris, took his turn standing watch one memorable night. He performed his security check then settled in his room across from the men's public restroom. When he heard one of the urinals flush in the dead of the night he "didn't even get out of bed. Well, yes I did, only to make sure the door was locked. My feet went cold." he said. During another inspection, Pete noticed a light left on in one of the cottages. To his astonishment he discovered that the light emanated from *behind* the refrigerator. To extinguish the light, Pete needed to move the heavy appliance to remove the light bulb from its fixture in the alcove.

Even the ladies' restroom possessed other-worldly goings on. A female employee always accused others of placing a chair behind the door in the lounge. She became so upset over the invasive and pervasive incidents that she finally quit her job. Assuredly no one (in the flesh) working there caused the entrapment.

In the dining area, the sound of children's footsteps running across the floor resound. Could this sound be an echo of Preston and his brothers' boyhood antics? (One of his brothers also committed suicide). Another odd anomaly is the large swinging kitchen doors sometimes move back and forth as if being pushed by unseen hands.

During renovations, evidence of Preston's handiwork appeared in nearly every building. His signature and the date of the job autographed the wood and walls. He's left his ghostly signature as well in photos taken in Knollwood Cottage. One snapshot clearly shows a shadowy male figure on the rustic staircase when no one else was in the building. Spirits manifest in some photographs because cameras detect a broader spectrum of light energy than the human eye. All who studied the image agreed it must be Preston.

During the summer of 1999 Preston's wife passed away. At the funeral, one of their children said, "Guess Pop will leave you alone now." Since then, nothing inexplicable has occurred. Well, except that the sprinkler system activated during the winter for no explainable reason. The Convention Hall building flooded causing $44,000.00 in damage. Preston's last revenge it's hoped.

SARANAC LAKE

STEVENSON
MEMORIAL COTTAGE

*Chosen good ones, brewed best
aroma of this black coffee so crisp,
haunts me in a night's fright
of tormenting silence throughout the night!*
—Inner Whispers, *A Black Coffee's Chill*

D r. Edward Livingston Trudeau was diagnosed
with tuberculosis in 1873. The conventional
thinking of the times suggested a change of climate.
He went to live in the Adirondack Mountains,
initially at Paul Smith's Hotel, spending as much
time as possible in the great outdoors. Fortunately,
he subsequently regained his health. In 1876 he
moved his family to Saranac Lake and established a
medical practice.

In 1882, Trudeau read about a Prussian
physician's success treating tuberculosis with the
"rest cure" in cold, clear mountain air. Inspired

by these positive results, Trudeau founded the Adirondack Cottage Sanitarium for treating TB. His fame helped establish Saranac Lake as a healing mecca. Author Robert Louis Stevenson became one of Trudeau's early patients.

Robert Louis Stevenson was a Scottish novelist, poet, essayist and travel writer. His best-known books include *Treasure Island*, *Kidnapped*, and *The Strange Case of Dr. Jekyll and Mr. Hyde*. A literary celebrity during his lifetime, Stevenson occupied Baker Cottage from October 1887 to April 1888. Twenty years earlier, Adirondack guide Andrew Baker built the house overlooking the Saranac River near Moody Pond as a residence. He later adapted the structure for use as a cure cottage by adding the west wing. While under Dr. Trudeau's care, Stevenson wrote a number of essays including the *Master of Ballantrae.* The Stevenson Society of America purchased the dwelling in the 1920s to house the author's memorabilia.

Even though his good friend William Henley wrote of Stevenson, "a spirit intense and rare," Stevenson's spirit is not the one who infiltrates the cottage.

Mike Delahant is a third-generation resident curator whose grandmother once proclaimed, "We're not the only ones living here." The museum caretakers discern a palpable sadness and attribute the sorrowful sensation to Mrs. Baker. The Bakers lived into their eighties but were pre-deceased by their five children. Nothing is more powerful than the bond between a mother and child. Losing a child is a mother's worse nightmare—losing five is unfathomable. No mother can recover from such terrible losses without imprinting grief on her environment.

One spirit who did make his presence known to Mike is "Old Quizzey." Mike says Quizell was one of Saranac Lake's resident characters. He is best remembered for the zoo he established next to his live bait shop in town. Old Quizzey lived next door to the Baker cottage. One day when Mike broke his coffeepot, he asked his next door neighbors if he could borrow one of theirs. The neighbors had one on hand that belonged to a former tenant—Old Quizzey. Mike used the aluminum percolator until he bought a new coffeemaker. Quizzey's percolator remained overlooked on the stove awaiting its return. One morning as Mike walked through the kitchen the pot flew off the stove, onto the table and then to the floor. Mike surmised Old Quizzey *really* needed his morning cup o' joe!

Requiem

Under the wide and starry sky,
 Dig the grave and let me lie.
 Glad did I live and gladly die,
 And I laid me down with a will.

This be the verse you grave for me:
 Here he lies where he longed to be;
 Home is the sailor, home from sea,
 And the hunter home from the hill.
—Robert Louis Stevenson, *Underwoods*

HAUNTED CURE COTTAGE

Some men would quell the thing with prayer
Whose sightless footsteps pad the floor,
Whose fearful trespass mounts the stair
Or bursts the locked forbidden door.
—Robert Bridges, *Low Barometer*

Between 1873 and 1945, Saranac Lake flourished as a world-renowned center for the treatment of tuberculosis. The cure therapy exposed patients to fresh air and mandated complete bed rest. Conifer trees exude a turpentine scented fragrance that permeates the atmosphere and purifies the air. The presence of this restorative balsam-scent assisted in the healing of many patients.

During this era, a specific style of building emerged, the "cure cottage." Many of these dwellings still exist, their value recognized by 63 listings on National Register of Historic Places. These structures sheltered the sick and far too often witnessed their death. Some remain possessed by spirits. One in particular was spotlighted on Syfy channel's *Paranormal Witness* television program.

Property developer Mike Todd became captivated with an old rambling home in Saranac Lake. Even though the house on the hill possessed a haunted reputation Mike remained unfazed by the stories. When he started remodeling the building, however, he began to rethink his mindset. As soon as he purchased the "fixer-upper," he set to work so he could quickly rent out the first and second floor apartments. The third floor was completely gutted and full of junk so Mike decided to save that space for last. He resided on-site while he worked on the building. On his first night of work, he placed his drill on the floor for a moment, reached back for it, but the tool was gone. Then the bathroom light flickered. Mike went to investigate, found nothing, and returned to his project. Lo and behold—there sat the errant drill sitting in the middle of the floor.

When first in the downstairs laundry room, Mike spied a pair of legs sprint past the doorway and up the stairs. He chased the transparent figure to the third floor. The trespasser quickly rounded the corner. Mike heard a closet door slam and when he reached the door and opened it he found only a pile of junk.

Mike's first tenant was Cynthia Warwick Seiler, a realtor who fell in love with the place. One night she ventured downstairs to do laundry accompanied by her dog Buddy. As she stuffed the washing machine the canine tore up the staircase. Cynthia followed Buddy to the third floor which felt ice cold. Buddy pawed at the third floor door. Every time Cynthia did laundry Buddy routinely ran up the stairs. One time, however, Cynthia felt certain someone stood behind her. She turned around slowly and came face-to-face with an apparition. Terrified, she raced outside, looked back at the house and spotted two unusual children in a third floor window.

One night as he tried to sleep, Mike heard footsteps walking toward the bed and spied a little ghostly girl on the other side of the glass doors.

As Mike showed an apartment to Jodi Gagnon, the prospective tenant felt something on her leg, as if a child tugged at her. She looked but saw nothing there. Ignoring the feeling, Jodi rented the apartment. Her tenancy ended when a six foot-tall phantom walked through her flat and into the pantry.

Veronica Montes and her son Ashton moved into another apartment. One day, as they sat in their home a definite chill filled the room. Veronica dismissed the sensation as a breeze. One day, as Ashton washed his hands he screamed for his mother because a strange boy occupied their bathroom. Veronica found no one there but soon saw a rubber ball roll through the apartment, out into the hallway and stop at the top of the stairwell. Then the ball deliberately rolled down the stairs one step at a time.

Mike soon learned about the influx of tubercular people to Saranac Lake at the turn of the 20th century and discovered his house once served as a cure cottage. Allegedly, more than 100 people died from the disease in the building. He eventually came to understand the spirits wanted the home's history honored and their presence as well. Psychics intuited the spirits' needs concurrently with Mike's realization. As a peace offering, the owner dedicated a small portion of the third floor to the lost souls. The offering calmed the house down considerably.

On the floor are mysterious footsteps,
There are whispers along the walls!
—Henry Wadsworth Longfellow, *The Haunted Chamber*

The Ohio Researchers of Banded Spirits (ORBS) paranormal group investigated the property. The Animal Channel featured the team's investigation on *The Haunted.* The "Touch of Death" episode showcased the Ohioans who utilized a night-vision camera, radiation detectors, electromagnetic-field detectors, thermal imaging, digital thermometer and digital voice recorders during their research. They also used a "soul sensor," one of their inventions that when activated, sounds an alarm and flashes LED lights.

The crew set out crayons and a box of Cracker Jacks to entice the ghostly children to interact. Remarkably, the temperature on the Cracker Jacks started to rise and investigator Chris Page gave the entity permission to open the box if it wanted to. "As plain as day, the spirit said 'no.' Why would a box of Cracker Jacks start heating up—it's just not normal," he said to reporter Robin Caudell of *The Press Republican*. The team went on to capture a child's ghostly handprint on a wall using thermal imaging.

The investigators strongly felt someone watched them particularly when in the basement. After they unscrewed a light bulb to create darkness for their equipment's functionality they heard a deep voice say, "There you go." *Every* time they asked a question about how the spirits died and/or about tuberculosis, a high-pitch noise resounded in response. The Ohio researchers labeled the cure cottage the creepiest place they've ever been.

ELIZABETHTOWN

ADIRONDACK HISTORY
CENTER MUSEUM

They'd charged him with the old, old crime,
And set him fast in jail:
Oh, why does the dog howl all night long,
And why does the night wind wail?
—Paul Laurence Dunbar, *The Haunted Oak*

Henry Deletnack DeBosnys hanged April 27, 1883 at the Elizabethtown courthouse. Convicted of murdering his wife and sentenced to death, DeBosnys became the last man to hang in Essex County. The execution became the talk of the town and citizens speculated the mysterious stranger arrived in Elizabethtown with an agenda. They suspected he purposely wooed the pretty widow, Elizabeth Wells, to claim her fortune as his own. The prosecutor argued this as the prime motive for her murder.

DeBosnys lured his wife of two months to a

hiking trail where he slashed her throat *and* shot
her for good measure. Her murder left her three
children orphaned. Witnesses observed DeBosnys
secreting Elizabeth's body under leaves at the side
of a dirt road. He adamantly denied his guilt but a
jury took only ten minutes to convict him.

The supposed soldier of fortune bragged he
traveled the world. He even boasted about his
service in the U.S. 7th Cavalry under Colonel George
Armstrong Custer at the Battle of Little Bighorn. Not
one of his tall tales was ever proven.

DeBosnys may have committed other crimes
according to Lindsay Pontius the Museum Educator
at the Adirondack Museum History Center where

his skull and the noose that snagged him are among related memorabilia on display. He allegedly killed a laundress before relocating to the North Country. With his cranium on parade, is it any wonder his restless spirit still skulks about the former school building at 7590 Court Street?

Museum Director Margaret Gibbs said summer intern, Jessie Olcott, witnessed DeBosnys' ghoulish specter. Ironically, Jessie later learned one of her ancestors sanctioned the criminal's hanging. Did the brazen killer appear to the young woman out of disdain for her forebear? Since no one else witnessed his wraith perhaps Jessie somehow possessed a psychic connection.

Another baffling incident occurred when staffers found a copy of a newspaper clipping about the murder case in the copy machine tray yet the original article was not on the copier's glass. This incident occurred prior to Jessie's knowledge of a family connection to the crime. Museum workers pondered over who and how the document copied. The original was kept under wraps for years because there was no reason to retrieve it. As they deliberated, the lights blinked out.

Before his execution, DeBosnys sold his body to a local physician for $15 in exchange for a suit to wear on the day of his execution. The hardcore narcissist wanted to impress his audience until his dying day. The doctor dissected the man's body and donated the skeletal remains to a local school. All that remains today is the skull preserved in the museum along with the spirit of the shameless psychopath.

THE DEER'S HEAD INN

All was quiet, nary a sound.
Yet there seemed to be something around.
The halls were vacant, the rooms quite bare
but the presence of something was always there.
—Edwina Reizer, *Ghost in a Haunted House*

In 1808 the Simmond's Cottage was built to accommodate North Woods' travelers. When the building sustained damage during a fire 20 years later, what remained of the structure was moved to the Deer's Head Inn's present site on Court Street opposite the Essex County Courthouse. Rebuilt as the Mansion House, the hostelry prospered for 40 years and then became the Deer's Head Inn.

The lodging supported troops during the War of 1812 when Army personnel commandeered the building for use as a hospital. Not only did those injured in the Battle of Plattsburgh find shelter, for a time, the structure also served as a school.

During Prohibition the Deer's Head's owner concealed his liquor inventory under the porch. The safely ensconced cache could only be accessed through a hidden door. When the porch underwent repair in 1991, a number of bottles turned up. They remain on display above the bar.

Two U.S. Presidents lodged at the Deer's Head. The signatures of Grover Cleveland and Benjamin Harrison appear in the inn's register. Another notable guest was abolitionist John Brown's widow who spent the night as her husband's body lay in state at the nearby courthouse.

Joanne Baldwin, one of the inn's owners, doesn't spend a lot of time tracking down the paranormal at her restaurant but she feels the place accommodates at least one ghost. She hears the spirit's disembodied footsteps upstairs. Might the elusive entity be a 19th

century soldier? Or a long-term guest who refuses to leave? Even a few diners observed the spirit but second-guessed their visions.

Every day it seems something inexplicable occurs according to Joanne. For instance, crumbs will be swept off the table and upon returning with the place settings the crumbs are back! Or a glass of wine will be poured, the bottle replaced behind the bar and when the bartender goes to serve the glass of wine it's not there! It's happenings such as these that gives one pause...

She spoke about a former server who was not exactly a "team player." The worker only looked out for herself and exuded a strange vibe. The restaurant's spirit seemed to take exception to her as well because the young woman inexplicably provoked the phantom's ire. Sometimes the kitchen's swinging door became impassable—no matter how hard she pushed, the door would not budge. The portal refused to open which made it impossible for her to perform her job on those occasions.

Catering to guests for over 200 years, the Deer's Head Inn endures as "the Adirondack's Oldest Inn." An ancient structure with a long human history— the perfect combination for a haunted setting.

HAND HOUSE

There came a footstep climbing the stair;
Some one standing out on the landing
Shook the door like a puff of air.
—Christina Rossetti, *The Ghost's Petition*

In 1861, Marcia Hand married at her father's home. She died nine months later at the age of twenty-five. Her father, Judge Augustus "A. C." Hand, lawyered for forty-seven years, served in Congress as a state senator and as a judge in the New York State Court of Appeals. They lived in Elizabethtown, in a brick Greek revival home built in 1849. Judge Hand commissioned the five-bedroom home on River Street where original artifacts still occupy the house—a beaver top hat, leather-bound books and a hide-covered hobbyhorse are among the belongings of five generations of the Hand clan. Another vestige is the spirit of a young woman— possibly Marcia or her sister, Ellen, both of whom died young.

The Bruce L. Crary Foundation grants scholarships to area students and since 1979 has owned the historic home listed on the National Register of Historic Places. Hannelore Kissam served as the foundation's Executive Director for 23 years and possesses firsthand knowledge of inexplicable incidents in the house. "Little things happen all the time," she proclaimed. Hanne said when Franciscan Friars attended a nearby ordination they stayed at the Hand House. During the night, one of the young men awoke to the sound of footsteps outside his bedroom door. Then the door opened and he soon felt someone sit on his bed and then lay on top of him! Terrified, he endured the pressure for several minutes until the invisible figure got up, opened the door and walked out. All the while his roommate in the adjacent bed slept like a log. The petrified cleric waited 'til dawn then raced to the rectory. He needed to talk a priest about the supernatural incident! He left the house that morning and never returned.

Hanna spent six weeks in the house recovering from surgery. She and her 11-year-old son stayed on the second floor. One night, at about 1:00 a.m. as her son slept in the next room, she heard a sound in the hallway. Then the doorknob turned. Hanne thought her son got up when she heard more noises out in the hall. With no reason to feel uncomfortable, she opened the door and spied a slight, dark-haired woman walk toward the servants' quarters, then *through* the door! As this strange event unfolded, Hanne noticed the large hallway mirror did not reflect the woman's image. On the contrary, at other times other staffers caught glimpses of phantom people in the mirrors when they entered empty rooms.

During the course of her workday, Hanne often perceived a presence, a spirit she described as "lost." The subtle encounter included "a whiff of human body odor masked with a flowery perfume." Not an offensive smell but more than we are used to people emitting today—personal hygiene standards differed over a hundred years ago. Most times she noticed this scent near the dining room where a portrait of Ellen Hand now hangs. Judge Hand's other daughter was a petite brunette who passed away at 32 years of age shortly after her marriage.

A home, or any place where people devote so

much time, is potentially ripe for haunting because the inhabitants' energy is implanted on the location. Former occupants feel comfortable amid the familiar furnishings of their earthly abode. How and why their energy manifests as spirits remains a mystery. Perhaps the energy of both women stays behind in the Hand House living out their interrupted lives.

STONELEIGH B & B

Little Ghost Cat
Flitting thru the house
On lightning fast
Little ghost feet
More silent than a mouse.
—Renee Hartman, *Little Ghost Cat*

Castle-like Stoneleigh B & B nestles cozily in the woods off River Street. The soothing sound of trickling Barton Brook creates a tranquil ambiance guests enjoy. The inn is a peaceful get-a-way where six inviting fireplaces entice visitors to cuddle up with a good book. Although it looks haunted from the outside, the inn is purr-fectly spirited.

Judge Francis Smith and his wife, Julia Scott Smith, bought Stoneleigh in 1884. H. H. Richardson's architectural style inspired the distinctive dwelling which is designed to emulate an elegant European castle. The Smiths adopted a daughter, Louise. After her parents' death, Louise stayed in the stone home with her cats until she passed away in the 1950s.

The house once served as a nursing home. The
renovations required to repurpose the structure
obscured, and in some cases even destroyed, certain
unique architectural features. In 1969, when Ronald
and Rosemary Remington, and their daughter
Rebecca, regarded the empty place as a potential
home, layers of dust coated the interior spaces.
Ronald had reservations about buying the place but
Rosemary's vision saw beyond the awful overhaul
and sensed what lay beneath.

A big, gray tabby cat welcomed the family by
sitting in the library doorway. Ronald sought to
fetch the creature but he scooted away. Ronald
pursued the errant pet but couldn't find him. He
thought it odd the cat left no footprints on the dusty
floor... how did the puss even get into the empty
house?

They bought the place and day after day
focused on refurbishing. The cat became a fixture
silently staring from afar as the work progressed.
His presence confounded the couple. Who owned
this beast? None of the neighbors knew. Each time
Ronald searched for the kitty he failed in finding the
elusive feline. Within a few years the new owners
returned the place to its original splendor. Every
now and then Ronald noticed the tomcat sitting in
the driveway as if smiling his approval.

In 1987, Rosemary opened the house as a bed and breakfast inn. Occasionally a guest will ask if she owns a cat. Rosemary shakes her head and smiles knowing what will follow. Some lodgers claim to feel a cat jump on the bed and walk across their pillow during the night. Invariably the guests who the experience the visit find it comforting because it reminds them of their own pet left behind. Rosemary's phantom feline makes them feel right at home.

Rosemary believes the ghost cat is one of Louise Smith's beloved companions who remains earthbound. The lonely puss needs to find its way home—on the other side.

KEENE VALLEY

AUSABLE INN

And travellers, now, within that valley,
Through the red-litten windows see
Vast forms that move fantastically
To a discordant melody.
—Edgar Allen Poe, *The Haunted Palace*

K eene Valley boasts the highest Adirondack
peak and the picturesque valley of the AuSable
River's East Branch, scenic delights beckoning
visitors for decades. On mist-laden mornings,
paranormal possibilities seem plausible in the
vaporous vale.

Reporter Martha Allen of the *Lake Placid
News* posed the question to readers, "Is Keene
Valley haunted?" She answered the provocative
question unequivocally saying "the spirits walk the
woodland paths of the hills and mountains." Martha
knows a thing or two about ghosts and hauntings
since she once shared her living space with a playful

poltergeist. She contends the AuSable Inn is haunted basing her conclusion on research and personal experience.

The AuSable Inn exists as a comfortable, family style restaurant, bar, liquor store and lodge located in the heart of the Adirondacks. Martha reported that 30 years ago when the place operated as the Spread Eagle a couple lived in the main bedroom. They experienced electrical anomalies such as their lights, television and radio repeatedly switching on in the middle of the night for no reason.

Some AuSable Inn lodgers report the sound of disembodied footsteps outside their room going up and down the hall. Another oddity is that sometimes the shower turns on and off without explanation. Also, there are those who found themselves locked in or out of their rooms. Confounded employees claimed baseball caps inexplicably flew off the shelves and directly at them.

One evening, as Martha sat at the bar with a friend she felt an incorporeal presence brush by her. Using intuitive skills, she discerned the sensation was a young man passing her on his way toward the front door. When she turned to look at him, no one was there. Although she didn't mention the impression to her friend, a split second later Martha's friend glanced in the same direction as if to see who walked behind her validating Martha's perception.

Check out the AuSable Inn where you can grab a brew and perhaps a boo too.

PORT HENRY

MORIAH TOWN HALL

O'er all there hung the shadow of a fear,
A sense of mystery the spirit daunted,
And said, as plain as whisper in the ear,
The place is haunted.
—Thomas Hood, *The Haunted House*

The iron ore mining industry flourished
in the region from 1820 to 1971. Workers
mined, processed and shipped iron ore from Lake
Champlain to the world. Port Henry became a
booming transport terminal for the element essential
to producing nails, tools, cookware and stoves along
with the expanding railroad industry across America.

Moriah Town Hall is a French Second Empire
structure built in 1875 and the former Witherbee
Sherman Company headquarters. The mining
company's building, one of three historic structures
on Park Place, houses Port Henry's government
offices. Moriah Town Supervisor, Thomas R.
Scozzafava said odd goings-on occur in the building

particularly on the third floor. The upper floor is
essentially vacant and Tom describes the space as
an open floor plan with large ceiling lights that
once illuminated drafting tables utilized when the
building housed Republic Steel. Staffers working
at night in the building, including Tom, sometimes
hear phantom employees on the closed-off floor.
Barbara Brassard worked at the town hall for 13
years. She didn't believe in ghosts until she worked
at the old building and wouldn't dream of going
there alone at night. Barbara also claimed echoes
of the past resounded on the third floor where she
swore something supernatural resided there.

Barbara maintained "things were not quite right." Small items went missing. For instance, a toothbrush and paste she kept at work disappeared. What co-worker would swipe someone else's toothbrush? Files vanished for no explainable reason. When unusual incidents such as these occur over and over the culprit could be a poltergeist. A poltergeist is an earthbound spirit who is frustrated that no one seems to notice them. As a result they attempt to attract attention by making noises, moving or stealing things.

The *Press Republican* published a story about a ghostly male figure who peers out a third-story window. The specter, who they dubbed Fred, is thought to be an individual who died on-site when the mining company owned the brick building.

LEE HOUSE APARTMENTS

Once the largest hotel in Port Henry, the Italianate style Lee House on South Main Street opened across from the village green in 1877. The hostelry boasted 50 guest rooms and introduced one of the first Otis elevators. Saved from demolition, the building underwent renovation and today serves as senior citizen housing.

Some residents say they've spotted a specter in the halls. They say the apparition is someone who perished in the hotel during its heyday. Hallways are high traffic areas and therefore hold a lot of energy. These established pathways store the energy of days gone by and somehow replay it for us to see, hear or feel in the form of paranormal phenomena.

According to manager Stella Blaise, even newly arrived residents complain of hearing somebody walking up and down the corridor at night. Although Stella has worked at the housing complex for 14 years, she's yet to experience anything paranormal except for the residents complaining *all the time* of the relentless footsteps.

CROWN POINT

PENFIELD HOMESTEAD MUSEUM

Ghost Hunter, Ghost Hunter what have you found
Maybe someone's lost soul just floating around
With cameras in hand just and hoping to find
The existence of life, beyond yours and mine.
—Scott Wise, *Ghost Hunter*

Located in historic Ironville in the Town of Crown Point, the Penfield Museum is dedicated to preserving the history of the North Country's ironworking industry during the 19th century. Considered the "Birthplace of the Electric Age," the hamlet is the first industrial setting in the United States to utilize electricity.

The region supported the Union effort during the Civil War and exemplified modern manufacturing development. The Hammondville mines provided the iron ore which was separated in Ironville then shipped via railroad to Lake Champlain. The ore material was used in many wartime applications including the U.S. Navy's first ironclad steamship *U.S.S. Monitor.*

Created in 1962, the Penfield Foundation maintains six buildings, protects the historic landscape and preserves the Crown Point Iron Company and Penfield Family legacies. There's more than meets the eye at the Penfield homestead according to local historian Joan Hunsdon who volunteers at the site. All sorts of noises plague the house and furtive black figures lurk in the shadows. In the dining room, the teacup display is often found disturbed. One cup mysteriously finds its way closer to the fireplace along with a chair also repositioned by the hearth as if to accommodate the comfort of an unseen resident. Joan suspects the ephemeral occupant is Annie Penfield.

Miss Annie never married and she was the last Penfield to occupy, *still* occupy, the historic home. The museum depicts an earlier time that's familiar to her spirit and it appears she stays behind enjoying the comfortable ambiance. One volunteer felt a shove by unseen hands outside what used to be Miss Annie's bedroom. Clearly, the dowager wants her personal space respected.

Ghostly presences often affect electrical devices and at the Penfield homestead lights are found on when they were definitely turned off. Another strange anomaly is the icy cold atmosphere in the office which chills the bones even on the warmest summer days. Spirits sometimes draw energy from the physical environment which affects the temperature of small areas creating cold spots. At one time a former caretaker heard an altercation ensuing in the chamber. The sounds of loud male voices arguing and banging noises were heard yet what they said specifically was indiscernible.

A local paranormal group led by the Thatcher family investigated the property. Certain equipment failed to work but when taken out of the building functioned fine. Joan felt Miss Annie didn't like all these new-fangled gadgets. The ghost hunt turned up little—in fact, they found the place to be abnormally quiet!

Check out the annual Apple Folk Fest held the Sunday of Columbus Day weekend and explore 19th century living by visiting 703 Creek Road in historic Ironville. Miss Annie may invite you to share a cuppa!

TICONDEROGA

FORT TICONDEROGA

When all went quiet, still and sound
I raised myself up from the mound
Of horses hoof for they did pound of
The Ghost Rider passing by.
—Irina Whitford, *Ghost Rider*

Fort Ticonderoga is one of the most popular historic destinations in the Adirondack region.
When it comes to hauntings, the fortress possesses all the elements—apparitions, disembodied voices, phantom lights, ghostly drumbeats, droning bagpipes and spectral horses. Staff members report an 18th century soldier in both the officers' and soldiers' barracks and moving orbs of light. Some tourists report a specter sitting in an antique dining room chair. In the cemetery, people hear hoof beats, observe a figure on horseback and shadows moving about the grounds.

Ticonderoga translates to "the place between two rivers" in the Iroquois language. In the mid-1700s,

75

FORT TICONDEROGA

76

the site was called Fort Carillon and served as a trading post on the St. Lawrence and Hudson Rivers trade route. Considered the "key to a continent," the site connected Canada and New York. The British first conquered the French bastion and ultimately, Ethan Allen and his Green Mountain Boys from Vermont, along with Benedict Arnold, stormed the fort on May 10, 1775. Their surprise attack was the first successful act of aggression of the American Revolution. George Washington visited the fort in July 1783, presidents James Madison and Thomas Jefferson stayed there in July 1791.

The fortress lay in ruins for years. Many locals used the stones in building or reinforcing their homes. William Ferris Pell (1779–1840) was a New York City importer of mahogany and marble and the grandson of the third and last lord of Pelham Manor, a 50,000 acre estate encompassing today's northeastern Bronx and southeastern

Westchester counties. In 1820, Pell purchased the Fort Ticonderoga garrison grounds. In 1825, Pell's first summer home at Ticonderoga was destroyed by fire and The Pavilion was constructed on the same site the following year. He eventually transformed his summer home into a hostelry for travelers who visited the historic relic overlooking the Champlain Valley.

The bastion is a National Registered Historical Site, not-for-profit educational institution, and a museum holding the world's largest and most impressive cannon collection. The museum contains Washingtonian memorabilia and even a relic of Martha's wedding dress.

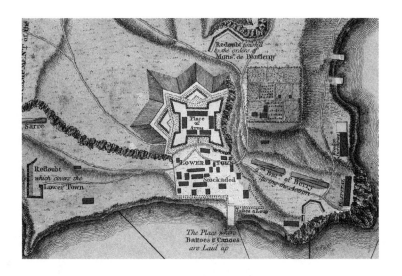

Visitors pass through iron gates and drive along a monument-lined road. The deadwood of centuries-old spruce hangs heavy over the site where in 1777 over three thousand lost their lives in battle. The bunkers marking the French battle lines are still evident. To honor the dead, Marquis de Montcalm erected a gigantic cross. Many sensitive visitors feel an extreme sense of sadness at the spot commemorated by a replica red cross.

Stories of strange phenomena and inexplicable occurrences transpired for decades and the fort's staff systematically collects and documents these stories. The historic site rates a listing in Dennis William Hauck's *National Directory of Haunted Places*. Hauck cites the ghostly appearance of one of the garrison's former commanders, General "Mad" Anthony

Wayne and his spurned sweetheart, Nancy Coates. Nancy committed suicide by walking into Lake Champlain when Wayne left her for another woman.

Lead interpreter John M. Rice claimed the site harbors lots of spirits. "One day many re-enactors mustered at the fort. One stood alone. I went over to introduce myself and poof, he disappeared," he said. Another time while standing in the dining hall Rice noticed a grayish haze form into a soldier sporting large blue cuffs typical of a French soldier's uniform. Rice remained mesmerized and continued to watch the Frenchmen's specter walk right through a door! He also observed a casement window move of its own accord. Rice explained most of the sightings occur on mist-laden days when the atmosphere is thick. The spirits draw energy from the ether in order to manifest. Rice also shared the story of three clairvoyant women who visited the popular tourist attraction. As a fife and drum corps played a rousing call to arms, the women observed *dozens* of spirits mobilize into action. The trio became so upset at the sight of the vision they immediately left in tears. People often feel an overwhelming sadness or an uncontrollable urge to cry, "Some can't even make it through the door," he said.

I interviewed the late Ruth Fitzgerald in front of the "Ladies from Hell" diorama depicting a scene of Duncan Campbell's Black Watch Regiment. The octogenarian appeared in a televised documentary about the haunted fort. Fitzgerald said she used to tend the King's Farm on the property's lower road. One afternoon she distinctly heard a galloping horse. Fearing one of the horses escaped she rushed outside and stood awestruck amid the dust cloud caused by the stampeding phantom. Fitzgerald said she could feel the breeze on her face and wind through her hair on the perfectly still day.

Another oddity is a small orb of light zipping around the top floor of the barracks building. "Several of us see it," said Fitzgerald. Also, "In the morning, there's the sound of someone walking before the museum opens to visitors." When the crumbling front wall needed restoration the phantom pacing became more prevalent. Perhaps indicating the spirit's anxiety over the ruptured wall and the possibility the fortress could be breached.

When I asked another interpreter, Beverly O'Neil, if she experienced anything out of the ordinary, she replied, "Of course there are the footsteps in the morning." O'Neil continued to tell the tale of a young Native American girl who leaped to her death rather than submit to an officer's improper advances. Her lonely earthbound spirit drifts along the shoreline.

Born and raised in Ticonderoga, O'Neil is a longtime fort employee. At daybreak one morning, she heard the distinctive beat of drums in the distance. She remembered re-enactors were scheduled at the fort to commemorate an important anniversary, so she roused herself to prepare for the day. Bev told several of the visiting musicians that she heard them practicing at sunrise. They seemed surprise because they didn't start playing until after 8:00 a.m. Who drummed at dawn's first light? Bev O'Neil feels she knows because she holds a special connection to the fort and its rich haunted history.

The Atlantic Paranormal Society (TAPS) investigated Fort Ticonderoga's long history of ghostly activity for the Syfy Channel's popular series *Ghost Hunters*. In the pitch-black cemetery of unmarked graves, the research team observed a figure walking in the woods and discerned whispering. As they talked to the furtive form the electromagnetic field readings rose on their detectors. This spike indicated a presence yet the heat thermal signature showed no indication of a living entity.

In the attic of the officers' barracks, the ghost hunters observed a bright flashing light and heard moaning and breathing. In the enlisted men's quarters they discerned what sounded like someone coughing.

The Legend of Duncan Campbell

T he most widely known Fort Ticonderoga ghost
story is the haunting tale of Duncan Campbell.
The Scottish nobleman died on July 18, 1758, after
suffering wounds sustained while battling French
forces at Fort Carillon. The fort was later renamed
Fort Ticonderoga by the British. Actually several
ghostly legends arose with the Scotsman.

A number of years before his death, while laird
of Inverawe Castle, Campbell sheltered a stranger
who turned out to have killed Campbell's cousin,
allegedly in self-defense. Faced with the conflict
between betraying his guest or exacting vengeance
for his cousin's death, Campbell compromised by
allowing the killer to hide out in a nearby cave. His
cousin's infuriated ghost appeared to Campbell
and ominously promised to meet him again at
Ticonderoga, a place then unknown to Campbell.

Campbell's Black Watch Highland Brigade
arrived in America and mustered at Fort Carillon
in the northeast wilderness. Only when Campbell
arrived at the front line did he learn the alternate
name for the fort, *Ticonderoga*.

In the haze of battle, his cousin's ghost appeared

again and ominously reminded him, *at last we meet at Ticonderoga*. Campbell realized his fate and awaited his cousin's retribution. Legend says the battle was replicated in the clouds over Inverawe Castle in Scotland on the afternoon of the attack. Campbell died nine days later from his wounds and was buried near the fort. Disinterred in the mid-19th century, his remains now lay alongside Jane McCrea, also a war casualty, in Fort Edward's Union Cemetery.

The story of the ghostly prediction and the apparition in the clouds over Inverawe are oft told tales. To further the legend, they say on stormy nights the two cousins appear at Fort Ti pacing its ancient battlements.

Be sure to explore more of the fort's ghostly past during evening Garrison Ghost Tours held throughout the season.

The muffled drum's sad role has beat
The soldier's last tattoo
No more on life's parade shall meet
Those brave and fallen few.
Rest on embalmed and sainted head
Dear as the blood ye gave
No impious footstep here shall tread
The herbage of your grave.
—Theodore O'Hara, *The Bivouac of the Dead*

UPPER JAY

WELLSCROFT LODGE

Day dreaming-filled
And heart in the air
For the lady in red,
For words never said.
—Tee'k Aminu, *Lady in Red*

The Wellscroft Lodge was built in 1903 as a summer estate for Jean and Wallis Craig Smith of Michigan. The Smiths enjoyed the home for many years until they lost their fortune in the 1929 stock market crash.

The most recent owners, Linda and Randolph Stanley, ran the 1890 Tudor Revival mansion as a bed and breakfast inn. During their residency, the house possessed friendly spirits. Although no radio existed on the property, guests often discerned gentle, instrumental melodies emanating from different parts of the house. Disconcerting murmurings were heard, although indistinguishable. Most mysterious was the "lady in red" apparition spotted gazing out the front window or gliding down the staircase.

At the time of its construction upon Ebenezer Mountainside, the Wellscroft Lodge was one of the largest estates built in the Adirondacks. Its English Tudor style was modeled after a Scottish home the Smiths admired. The 17,000 square foot manse included a community of buildings to support the family's every imaginable need. An all-important caretaker's house existed along with the power house, ice house, carriage house and stables. Gardens, a children's playhouse, golf course and even a maple syrup house buoyed the enclave.

Given the couples' iron-ore and timber industry fortune, no expense was spared.

Like so many others, the 1929 economic downturn squelched the Smith's lavish existence. Sold in 1942, various owners possessed the massive property over the next 50 years. The structure saw incarnations as a private home, a public resort and eventually sat abandoned. The sadly neglected home that once housed genial family gatherings and convivial parties became the victim of vandals.

The Stanleys took on the onerous task of restoring the great house to its original splendor. During their residency as innkeepers guests often mentioned to their hosts how they enjoyed the beautiful music piped through the rooms. Visitors also often heard the noise of disembodied revelers coming in the front door along with the distinct sound of the heavy, creaking door opening and closing. Stanley family members and workers hired to help with the restoration also experienced supernatural anomalies. One of the painters never returned to finish the job because he was so freaked out. The painter's behavior is in contrast to a caretaker's spirit who stays behind long after the completion of his earthly tasks. His ghost is spotted outside traipsing between the fire house and the power house. He is recognized by his unusual wide-brimmed hat. Another spirit sighted is a former servant who stands with his arms crossed at the entrance to the third floor servants' quarters.

Without doubt the Lady in Red is the star of this haunted house. Her ghost glides down the grand staircase and passersby observe her eerie presence peering out a second floor window of the "green room" as well. Her appearance identifies her as a turn-of-the century Victorian woman. Mrs. Stanley actually noticed physical impressions on the window seat cushions left by the ethereal lady of the house. When Mrs. Stanley contacted a psychic medium, the clairvoyant immediately discerned a woman in a red dress sitting by the window watching and waiting for someone.

The well-crafted Wellscroft Lodge offers breathtaking views, incomparable serenity and remarkable presences from the past.

A form sits by the window,
That is not seen by day,
For as soon as the dawn approaches
It vanishes away.
—Henry Wadsworth Longfellow, *The Haunted Chamber*

WESTPORT

THE LAST GOODBYE

Yet ghosts there are; and they blow, they blow,
Out in the wind and the scattering snow.-
When I open the windows and go to bed,
Will the ghosts come In and stand at my head?
—Frances Stearns Davis, *Ghosts*

When the Northern Canal opened in 1823 linking Lake Champlain and the Hudson River, new ways of making money stimulated the creation of a unique watercraft to meet the rising trade. The Lake Champlain sailing-canal boat was invented. Designed to sail on the lake like a sailboat, upon reaching the canal, the centerboard raised and the mast lowered, transforming the vessel into a canal boat for towage on the canal. Finding the shipwrecked *Troy* in 2000 was a major event in marine archeology. The momentous discovery brought to light the design of this historic vessel. The wreck appeared remarkably intact with its bow embedded in the lake bottom.

The *Troy* disappeared on her maiden voyage to Westport in 1825 during a November gale. Five young men and boys sailed the vessel loaded with iron ore for the newly established iron furnace. Twenty-five-year-old Jacob Halstead skippered the schooner that carried his 13-year-old brother, George, his stepbrother Jacob Pardee and two crewmen, Daniel Cannon and John Williams. A gale engulfed the ship and archeological evidence supports the theory that the heavy cargo shifted during the tumultuous storm causing the vessel to sink very quickly.

Back at home on Halstead Hill, the boys' mother and sisters sat at home waiting… In *History of Westport, Essex County, New York,* Caroline Royce wrote they were:

> "listening through the storm for the sound of homecoming footsteps as the night wore on. Suddenly they heard the boys on the doorsteps, stomping off the snow in the entry as they were wont to do before coming in. The women sprang to the door and opened it, stepped to the outer door and looked down upon the light carpet of untrodden snow which lay before it, and then crept trembling back to the fireside, knowing that son and brothers would never sit with them again within its light."

ADIRONDAC

THE DESERTED VILLAGE

The Adirondack Mountain region is rich in myth and legend and two men actively preserved the folklore. For many years, Henry Van Hoevenberg operated the Adirondack Lodge on the outskirts of Lake Placid. Most nights Van Hoevenberg recounted captivating tales in front of a roaring campfire. Author Seneca Ray Stoddard published many of these stories in his *Northern Monthly*.

One story concerns the ghost town of Adirondac that exists near the headwaters of the Hudson River. Ramshackle houses still dot the landscape along with pieces of rusty equipment half buried in the woods. Theodore Roosevelt traveled to the settlement in 1901. A few days before his arrival, the vice-president visited President William McKinley who was recovering from a gunshot wound sustained in Buffalo. Roosevelt was a few hours into his hike up Mount Marcy when a local man made the climb carrying a telegram announcing the president's grave condition. Soon after, the VP learned McKinley passed away making Roosevelt the 26th President of the United States.

In early 1830, Archibald McIntyre unearthed rich iron ore deposits here and by 1832, a company town formed near Tahawus. Forges were built to extract the iron from the magnetite ore. First called McIntyre, the town was later renamed Adirondac in 1848 by the U.S. Postal Service when a post office opened at the remote location.

In 1845, iron works manager David Henderson was accidentally killed by his own pistol while surveying ways to harness more water power for the mining operation. In 1856, a flood washed away fifty percent of the site. McIntyre died two years later, in 1858, triggering the works' permanent shut down.

In 1873, Seneca Ray Stoddard described the deserted village of Adirondac in his popular guidebook, *The Adirondacks*. The November 7, 1907 edition of *The Elizabethtown Post and Gazette* contained an abbreviated version of Stoddard's story, entitled "The Forsaken Village," which started the haunting rumors.

According to the legend, a New York businessman traveled to the Adirondacks for a vacation. Along the way, he happened upon the remains of the abandoned village. Roaming about the ghost town he discovered a perfectly furnished house looking as if its occupants just up and left. Down the lane the businessman found the iron company's office. He lost himself in exploring the workplace and its ledgers left in the open safe. Before long darkness fell. Miles from anywhere, he returned to the furnished house and made himself at home for the night in one of the bedrooms.

Around midnight, he awoke to the sound of footsteps. An apparition appeared in the doorway who claimed he was the founder of the village. The ghost explained he was searching for a letter written to his daughter, Mina, by her artist boyfriend. He disliked the young man, sent him away and stopped all communication between them by hiding the boy's correspondence. When his daughter grew ill, the man searched in vain for the letter. Mina soon died of a broken heart and the father felt cursed to walk the earth until he found the missing letter.

The next morning, the sympathetic visitor searched the house and eventually found the missive in a hole in the wall. That night he placed the letter on the table in the house. The ghost showed up again because he awakened the sleeping man with a great cry of joy. When the businessman reached the table he saw the letter was gone.

Stoddard alludes to the incident in his famous guidebook. He recalled his own visit to Adirondac where his hosts provided lodging in one of the deserted houses that possessed a haunted reputation. The author confessed he did hear strange sounds throughout the night.

When it comes to tales of the supernatural, a fine line exists between fact and fiction.

AUSABLE CHASM

PHANTOM BRIDGE

And as the moon from some dark gate of cloud
Throws o'er the sea a floating bridge of light,
Across whose trembling planks our fancies crowd
Into the realm of mystery and night.
—Henry Wadsworth Longfellow, *Haunted Houses*

Ausable Chasm is one of America's oldest tourist attractions. The Ausable River runs through the sandstone gorge then empties into Lake Champlain. Rainbow Falls feeds the two-mile-long gorge dubbed the "Grand Canyon of the East." Formed nearly 500 million years ago during the Cambrian period, William Gilliland of County Armagh, Ireland is credited with discovering the natural wonder in 1765 as he explored the west coast of Lake Champlain.

In 1793, High Bridge became the first of many bridges to span the chasm. Huge Norway pines, laid bank to bank, crossed the great divide. Six, 20-inch-wide wooden girders supporting a plank roadway remained in use until 1810 or 1812. Perhaps the last person to traverse High Bridge was the legendary Max Morgan.

Mother Nature wreaks havoc with bridges constructed over the gorge. In January 1996, a sudden heat wave melted snow and record rainfall created a massive runoff. Enormous ice blocks tore through the chasm along with uprooted, 60-foot trees. Even trailers from a nearby campsite crashed through the chasm like tumbling toys. Seventy-foot steel bridges tore from their foundations and crashed down the cliffs. In November 1996, heavy rains destroyed five of Ausable Chasm's ten bridges, three of them new.

Several legends surround High Bridge, including Max Morgan's celebrated crossing. According to lore, in the 19th century a rain soaked Morgan burst into a local tavern. He settled in for a warm meal and declared with pride that he was surprised to see the bridge over the gorge still intact. His comment drew the attention of the patrons. The innkeeper eventually disputed the claim and informed Morgan that only one stringer, an 18-inch square beam, remained. Morgan chewed on this and went on to say he lived in the town 20 years ago and helped construct the overpass. The patrons chimed in stating the bridge was washed out years ago. Morgan resolutely replied he drove over the bridge en route to the tavern explaining he distinctly heard the horse's hooves as they struck the thick wooden planks and the thundering waters 125 feet below. An argument ensued and bets were made.

The next morning the entire town turned out at the old bridge site. Sure enough, in the sandy loam they spied the hoof prints leaving the girder and on up to the tavern. A surefooted lad walked across the narrow beam and saw horse prints leading up to the girder.

The townsfolk said angels carried him to the other side. Despite his good fortune, when the reality dawned on Morgan his jet black hair turned snow white. He trembled uncontrollably and the shakes plagued him for the rest of his life.

ACKNOWLEDGEMENTS

I sincerely thank the following
individuals for helping me
bridge the gap between an idea and a reality.

Joanne Baldwin
Deer's Head Inn

Stella Blaise
Lee House Apartments

Barbara Brassard

Joe Conto
Pete Harris
Jim Patterson
Whiteface Club

Karla & Mike Delahant, Curators
Stevenson Memorial Cottage

Brian Dominic
Century 21 Foote-Ryan Real Estate

The late Ruth Fitzgerald
Bev O'Neil
John M. Rice
Fort Ticonderoga

Margaret Gibbs
Adirondack History Center Museum

Joan Hunsdon
Crown Point Historian

Hannelore Kissam

The late Mary Mackenzie
Lake Placid Historian

Mary Pat Ormsby and Tony Carlino
Stagecoach Inn

Rosemary Remington
Stoneleigh Bed & Breakfast

Linda Roy
John Brown Farm

Thomas Scozzafava
Moriah Town Supervisor

The late Marilyn "Lyn" Witte

Special thanks to graphic designer
Deb Tremper of Six Penny Graphics

&

To Maryann Way
My loyal friend who wields the "blue pencil!"

BIBLIOGRAPHY

Aber, Ted. *Adirondack Folks*. Prospect Books, 1980.

Allen, Martha. "Is Keene Valley Haunted?" *Lake Placid News*; June 6, 2008.

Ballou, Eleen. "Haunting tale told of LP Club." Retrieved from: http://www.htn.net/lplacid/history/old_news/haunting%20tale.htm.

Caudell, Robin. "Saranac Lake cure cottage featured in 'The Haunted.'" *The Press Republican*, November 13, 2010.

Delarue, John. "The Adirondack's Oldest Inn." www.4peaks.com.

Farnsworth, Cheri. *Haunted Northern New York, Volume 4*. North Country Books, 2010.

Folwell, Elizabeth. "A Show of Hands, Capturing the spirit of a stately Elizabethtown home." Retrieved from: http://www.adirondacklifemag.com/blogs/2012/10/23/a-show-of-hands/.

Ghost Hunters. "Fort Ticonderoga." Season 6, Episode 2, March 10, 2010.

Granato, Sherri. "The Ghosts of Saranac Lake, New York." Retrieved from http://voices.yahoo.com/haunted-america-ghosts-saranac-lake-york-10845851.html?cat=16.

Hauck, Dennis William. *National Directory of Haunted Places*. Penguin Books, 1996.

"Ice Skating Season to Begin at Lake Placid on Saturday." *The New York Sun*, June 24, 1942.

Lee, Grace Per. "Stagecoach Inn." *Adirondack Life*, Volume XLIII, Number 7, 2012.

Little, Gordie. "Ghost story of old stands up to tests of time." *The Press Republican*, August 12, 2001.

Macken, Lynda Lee. *Adirondack Ghosts*. Black Cat Press, 2000.

_____. *Adirondack Ghosts II*. Black Cat Press, 2003.

_____. *Adirondack Ghosts III*. Black Cat Press, 2010.

Manchester, Lee. "The Resurrection of Wellscroft." *Adirondack Life,* September/October 2002.

_____. "Bidding adieu to 'the deserted village,' Part 1." *Lake Placid News*, March 24, 2006.

_____. "A tour of three historic Adirondack inns, rescued from oblivion." *Lake Placid News;* April 7, 2006.

McKinstry, Lohr. "Adirondack Haunts." *The Press Republican,* October 27, 2007.

Ortloff, George Christian. *A Lady in the Lake*. With Pipe and Book Publishers, 1985.

Paranormal Witness. "The House on the Lake." Season 3, Episode 12, August 28, 2013.

Pitkin, David J. *New York State Ghosts, Volume 1*. Aurora Publications; 2006.

_____. *New York State Ghosts, Volume Two*. Aurora Publications; 2008.

"Placid Reflections—Spooky Happenings in Upper Jay!" *Placid Thoughts,* Issue #003, October 7, 2007; www.lake-placid-area-guide.com.

Revai, Cheri. *More Haunted Northern New York*. North Country Books; 2003.

_____. *The Big Book of New York Ghost Stories*. Stackpole Books; 2009.

Riley, Howard. "A Sort of Ghost Story." *Adirondack Daily Enterprise,* October 24, 2008.

Royce, Caroline Halstead. *Bessboro, A History of Westport, Essex County, New York*, 1902.

Sausa, Christie. "Haunted Lake Placid: Six Historical Places Where They Say There are Ghosts…" Retrieved from: http://thefreegeorge.com/thefreegeorge/haunted-lake-placid/.

"Told in Adirondacks." *Elizabethtown Post and Gazette*, November 7, 1907.

WEBSITES

Adirondack History Network: www.adirondackhistory.org

Ausable Chasm: www.ausablechasm.com/History/stories.asp

Essex County Historical Society/Adirondack History Center
Museum: www.adkhistorycenter.org

Fort Ticonderoga: www.fortticonderoga.org

John Brown Farm State Historic Site:
www.nysparks.state.ny.us/historic-sites

Lake Placid: www.lakeplacid.com/do/history/

Penfield Homestead Museum: www.penfieldmuseum.org

Stoneleigh Bed and Breakfast: www.stoneleighbedandbreakfast.com

Wikipedia: www.wikipedia.com

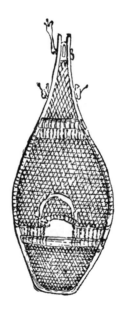

Other Haunted Titles
by Lynda Lee Macken

Adirondack Ghosts

Adirondack Ghosts II

Adirondack Ghosts III

Array of Hope, An Afterlife Journal

Empire Ghosts, New York State's Haunted Landmarks

Ghost Hunting the Mohawk Valley

Ghostly Gotham, Haunted History of New York City

*Ghosts of Central New York

Ghosts of the Garden State

Ghosts of the Garden State II

Ghosts of the Garden State III

Ghosts of the Jersey Shore

Ghosts of the Jersey Shore II

Haunted Baltimore

Haunted Cape May

Haunted History of Staten Island

Haunted Houses of the Hudson Valley

Haunted Lake George

Haunted Long Beach Island

Haunted Long Island

Haunted Long Island II

Haunted Monmouth County

Haunted New Hope

Haunted Salem & Beyond

*(originally published as *Leatherstocking Ghosts*)

Visit Lynda Lee Macken's website

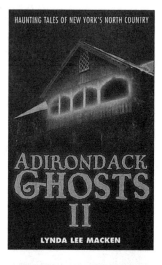

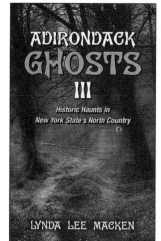

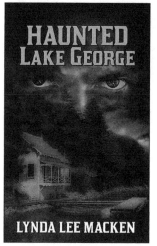

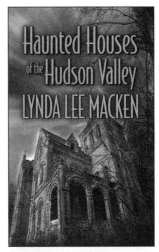